Hot Headed Si

Poetry.

Grace King.

<u>For</u>

The releasing of my feelings.
May you, the reader, always have the courage to love and nurture yours.

Contents

Acknowledgements

For illustrations:
Thank you to Daniel for the illustration designs for the poems: *To Be Vegan* and *Self-Love*. You have a generous spirit and are magically wired for design.
Thank you to Molli for the design for *Glitter*. It makes me happy that you have contributed to my written journey. You've captured the heart of my experience by relating with your own.
Seeing another's perspective of my work makes it bigger than what it is.

For experience:
Thank you to all the people that inspired these poems; without the compliment or contrast of your energy, I would know mine a little less.

For support:
Thank you to my mum. You keep me whole. Your love is healing; you give me room to be without judgement and that is so important to my health and wellbeing. Where I struggle to provide myself with a secure and loving space inside, I am lucky to have someone that I can trust to nurture me in that way. That is no small thing to honour and care for a wounded, vulnerable creature.
Thank you to my brother for being a listening ear and a fun-loving friend. The darkness I show to you is not an easy thing to see, but you only restore me with hope and wisdom.
Thank you to all the animals that awaken my guardian spirit. My love for you is wholesome and sharp. You teach me about my values and compel me to stand up for them.
Thank you to my friends who have read my poems in their rawness and encouraged me forward. Your loyal empathy gives me the strength to make the hard choices that best serve me. It amazes me how pure the love of friendship can be.
Thank you to my spirit guides for nudging me when it was time to leave a situation. When I've felt lost, your rare interjections have saved me from worser paths. My faith in you is more absolute than my faith in myself, but I know you give me room to balance that.

Introduction

Poetry is a language between your conscious mind and your soul. When used correctly, you can uncover secrets, wisdom, tools for survival and magic. Most importantly, you can learn self-love.

Often when we believe we have weaknesses, we are failing to see our strengths. I believe that when we view our qualities as the former, we're using our energy incorrectly, leading to self-sabotage and treacherous pathways. But when we view it as the latter through loving eyes, we can transcend ourselves to happiness with power and pride.

In my life, I've denied myself love and set my anchor to the opinions of others. This has made my journey scary, confusing, and directionless.

Poetry is designed so that deep, raw truths can exist outside of ourselves. They are the lifelines that can help us own our lives and take back control.

I think the best adventures begin when you become yourself; poems help me understand who that is.

Fell To Earth Again

I see the strain in your hazel eyes;
I'm distant and you don't know why,
But my heart left to fly with the shooting stars;
Where the moon and the night become who you are;

Alight, my tail lost fire;
But I was fuelled by my dreams;
They won't tire;

You're so innocent;
I'm so turbulent;
Our world's so full of depth;
Spells fall from my every breath;

But I lied to myself;
I can't just be friends;
Didn't think it would work;
Still got hurt in the end;

Stalling; my tail lost fire;
Staring at reality's eyes;

Now I feel the pain;
I fell to Earth again;
I singed the ground;
I'm all burned out,
As I've lost another friend.

Loneliness put his foot in the door;
But you, my dear, are not staying.

We Dance To Autumn's Song

Once the golden leaves of Autumn,
Accept they'll die;
They shine brighter;
Smoke and fire,
Will bring their last breaths to life.

There's a lady,
Who listens for the desperate stories,
Of scared thorns,
And pining roses;

She says it's the last of days,
Before a new world begins again;

When the duty is done;
Autumn skies can play,
And Autumn lands will sing;

It's a crunch of a leaf in the darkness;
It's the hesitant step,
And the short breath;
It's the fear of the stillness,
And the wind obsessing over secrets;

She pushes your bond to this;
And that's when it thrives,
With no promise of life;
A SHOT,
Without a gun.

I see colours;
My heart's a broken guitar string,
That's too excited for the pick;
I hear the grip of the passionate,
And I want to live without a template;

I want to be the crack of the whip;
The dashed dream behind the hatred.

And when the Autumn sings;
The brink of two worlds begins;

Black out;
No sun;
Artificial lights dance,
To Autumn's song.

Broken Watch

Is it time to let go?
Release the fear and pain...

Thinking you're easily replaced.
Then to stop yourself;
Get in your own way.

What's the worst that can happen?
The worst that did happen, coming round again.

But was it so bad? What makes it so bad?
That would be taking all the blame.

I think it's time to let go,
But to feel free is to be brave;
To fly through feels like laying your life lessons to waste.

Maybe it's OK,
Maybe you're lovable, anyway.

Queen Of Clubs

Check the carpet;
Don't let it rise too high;
I don't like hiding places,
Or little white lies.

There's a castle with echoes;
Open hearts dancing in walls.
I belong there;
Where matches ignite with calls.

If we court,
I won't be upfront or guile;
I'll pull the drawbridge,
Before showing crocodiles;

I'll fire canons to test your fibre;
Glance at you from the tower;
Storm the gardens with my sword;
Guarding my own but never a coward.

We are all entitled to locks and chains.
I wish for yours to remain,
If it makes you feel safe.
But a secret passageway,
Without entry between us,
Is a narrow and lonely place.

I don't like covering up the stain on the floor;
I want to address it.
I can't pretend the walls aren't chalked;
If we don't live in reality, we're a performance.

Not being perfect is King;
I like my crown and club;
Trying not to fear connecting,
By letting my steps make a thud;

Hear them with me;
Acknowledge they happened.

Then we can build a castle,
Where echoes are chapels.

Unleashed

I want to be unleashed:

   Passionate kisses;
  Shouting wildly;
   Laughing from deep abysses;
   Caressing mildly;
   Dancing like a goon;
  Singing together, like howling at the moon;
  Learning each other's bodies;
   Responsive and jolly;
   But quiet days and nights stay a dream.
   A reader; a deep thinker; my pillar;
  I'll be your sweetener;
   Carry me to bed;
    I'll enter you head.
  Enhance each other's lives;
  Wondering how we ever got by;

Shall I kiss you goodnight?
   Don't hold back so I know you're mine...

Everyone Knows It But You

We've been avoided by flames,
And burned by ice;
We thanked God for the rain;
So we could see the light.

I wanted you to swim in the moonlit sea,
But you didn't want to join me.
You agreed to a midnight stroll in the woods;
Did the stars know I wanted to close the distance between us?

We weren't in the right place;
I waited for you;
Torn between your peace and my needs;
Only together, when reality lost its time to dreams;
And when I reached for you,
After pushing you away;
You forgot you did the same.

You've got amazing taste;
Your thoughts are not to waste;
You're worth a million times more than you give yourself credit for,
But that's not my choice to make.

I know I meant so much to you;
I think you loved me;
I loved you too.
But I didn't want to be a dream;
I wanted it to be real;
I shot out flares,
That neither of us could see;

It was hard to understand;
We tried our best;
There was one move left;
A King's last stand.

My mum put it best:
"We want to make dreams a reality, and reality like a dream."
I forget to achieve it but I deserve to receive;

I can forgive us though,
For our tried beliefs.

Your big heart hides its cordoned moon;
Self-belief is our vessel's fuel;
You're worth a million times more than you give yourself credit for;
Everyone knows it but you.

And when I reached for you,
After pushing you away,
You said things wouldn't be the same;

We've got the key to the world,
But sometimes the only way to know is to lose.

Bitter Sweet Truth

Hazel and green;
A connection to keep;

Repellent magnets falling in love;

Deep, deep wounds,
And stinging gloves;

Two babies in a bath;
Without soap or a cloth;

Obstacles couldn't define us,
But a lack of flow caused the clot;

A fiery moon with depths of Jupiter;
A fair-minded sun, with heart of dazzling colour;

The universe cried when it couldn't hold her,
But she cried when she fell through the pillar.

And when a collision broke the system of the Milky Way;
Aliens steered us out from the waste.

Lessons learned:
How to put my own needs first;
Live true to my vision;
How to let myself receive;
Trust my intuition;
How to get more from life and expand my knowledge;
How big of a capacity I have to love;
How everything we perceive is a choice;
How to own my own feelings and voice;
How to be a highly sensitive person,
And be spiritual and gentle;
How to be a warrior and strengthen before going mental;
How to write a poem of beauty and Grace;
How to let you go, my mirror soulmate.

My World

My Mother hears

      She doesn't judge;

Excruciating talks that haunt my conscience,
Become understandings of human nonsense.

My Mother feels

      She wraps me up;

When life is confusing and demands too much,
She offers solutions and a steady crutch.

My Mother believes

      She fills my cup;

Dreams and hard work that mean the world,
Are propelled by Mum's mind; her ideas unfurl.

My Mother loves

      She takes a step back;

With freedom, and magic, she lets me grow in the wild,
And through all of the pain, I'm the daughter who smiles.

The Muddy Puddle

From being inside a bursting bubble;
Hearing the film of water smash,
Into shoots of thunder;
Feeling it wash my feet away.
Now I'm dealing with the flooded pavement,
I'm sat on;
The bubble is far away.

It's taken a long time to get here;
How I hurt myself,
Not saying no;
How I despair for hurting others,
By avoiding saying so;

I want to go,
Where I am strong,
And know,
When to move on;
Where I can love myself enough to embrace silence,
Instead of forcing myself into the next stage of enlightenment;
Compassion is sought after;
For myself,
By myself;
Forgiveness is what I need.

I didn't mean to burn those bridges;
Sometimes I'm not sure what I believe.

Too much for you;
We pushed it for love;
We should have let it fall through;

I know what's changed in me:
The spark of a new flame;
I am beautiful;
I deserve to exist;
I repeat this to myself,
Time and time again.

I like being alone,
But not feeling isolated;
I like my own ways,
But not if they're alienating;

Learning to set boundaries,
And to have compassion for myself;
That's what's sought after;
May all this collateral be looked after;
Swept away to the nether;
If it's only me holding it still together,
Give me strength to do better;
Let me float as lightly as a feather;
Let me light the waters,
And be the helper;
If bridges are burned,
We can fix them together;
Let's have compassion.
That'll be our saviour.

Twin Flames

I recognised you when I saw you;
A connection of no name;
Your ease and charm enhanced you;
But your lack of zest defamed;

You never wanted the spotlight;
But your magnitude got bite;
The closer I got, the more I rebounded;
Are we mirrors meeting in this life?

Do you like me? I can't tell...
Your hand caught my back;
Perhaps you were under my spell.

I said 'just friends' when the etiquette was whack;
I thought our friendship was strong,
But fickle was that,
When she presented your crack;
My blueprints went dusty,
Abandoned in the back.

But still you seduce me;
Whispering, aching, and needing me dear;
Lean in, the song said, so sweet and clear;
A far off dream so near;

Your depth ignited my flame;
I'll warm you, but then you go away;
I'm cold now; guarded;
Our energies won't make friends;
Am I what you want?
She's got your time again.

I'll date someone else,
After meeting him, while wearing your gift on my necklace;
You're now just a soul I cherish.
He puts in the effort,
But the pull isn't the same;
'Shoulds' and manners embellished;

I'm strong alone again;

I let him go and forget your name;
I miss you both; I can't win this game;
I send him a poem of insensitive truth;
I send you the same; hiding in places of unspoken proof;
I want you in my life, but of what magnitude in reality?
I want to love without a template,
But now I know that's foolish in totality.

I go to Paris;
You speak my name;
I'd sent you a poem of self-retrieving reign;
You returned one of great acclaim;
I cry again;
You put the effort in; will it go somewhere this time?
Are you still around the girl who wants to call you 'mine'?

You're holding back;
The date has my nerves on end.
Who's arranging the next one then?

Am I meant to drive this?
Won't you have a say?
Have patience; you don't know what you want;
I'm teaching you;
Is this patronisation gaunt?
This is new for me though because I know what I want;
I thank you;
I regain;
No blame;
Here we go again;

Finally we move a little further;
Deep chats in your car;
You bring her up when I was starting to feel stars;
Insecurity lies in wait;
How long? How far?

The pace is slow;
How does it move at all?

We held hands;
A small glow;
I want to release it all;
For two souls who sink into one another,
Why can't we unfold?

I made mistakes;
You weren't to know;
Learning to love myself and let guilt go;
You live by duty;
A peaceful air;
Unsure of your steps;
Heavy care;

You had all the love and grace but we weren't steady;
I appreciated you but too intensely;
Couldn't love apart;
Couldn't love together;
Oh but I did love you;
I hope our souls are friends forever;

Was I a dream to you?
A promise with no effort?
Was I the devil to you?
Toying with your heart for what benefit?
If I'd have been true to my mind, I'd have not known you;
You were already in my heart but I couldn't move on without you;

Do I leave you behind or pull you up?
You're hurting, you're failing, "What is this love?" You're wailing;
I'm sorry for derailing;
From my path I was hesitating;
I gave up waiting;
I hope I haven't left you hating.

You say hot and cold; I apologize for that;
Couldn't find a spanner to fix my on-off tap;
We're two sides of the same coin;
Different people in the same hat;

Love and pain;

Growth and stubborn remain;
"I'll fight but she keeps running away."
"Does she love me, does she not?"
I'm waiting for you to show up.

I let you go first while forgetting myself;
I blame you for not being selfless;
You're not selfish though;
The basics of the relationship weren't set.

You allow me to breathe nonsense;
Then ask me to make you clean;
But still you pollute the air and disappear;
Security to intrusion with no in-between;

I'm alone, wasted love, waiting to move;
Explanations meet push and pull;
If expectations aren't met are we incompatible?
I love him but I have to let him go;
My intuition told me so.

I wrote down my boundaries to be clear to myself;
The board toppled over; the pieces froze;
Heartbreak all over; no time to moan;
A heartfelt goodbye; leave me alone.

Remember The 60s?

I know you don't want me to prolong it,
And I thought I felt you try and sever it;
This psychic bond between us;
I'm lingering on its echoes and murmurs;

Eleven long days since we've broken;
Six since we've spoken;
Twenty since seeing each other in person;

I can't seem to go long;
I will soon, but a part of me's clinging on;
I know I should stop, and the universe eased us apart;
So what's with this bond like gold string tied around my heart?

I'll forget you one day but let me leave my two cents;
I'll write down my pipe dreams in a romantic sequence;
But I won't be able to tell the difference,
Between a lost truth and nonsense,
So pay attention please,
For this is the life we stood a chance:

Your hands are like a child's;
They make me sappy, caring and warm;
What's in your eyes?
Are you happy?
Why are you hiding?
I wish I could protect you from all storms.

You laugh like a hippy;
We fight but it's silly;
Stop the fuss; leave everything else;
Let's be together and forget the norm.

Your eyelashes are as long as mine;
Your eyes of stunning woodland colour;
Don't neglect your body,
I know of its incredible power;
I bet we made it in the years of the flower;
You dismiss your lungs but protect your liver;

Admit your beauty and go buy a mirror.

I can see us now;
Field walks and daisies;
All love and dreams;
Psychedelic lifestyles;
Animal rights, go green!

You're lost in yourself but you won't forget about me;
I'm your every waking thought;
Open your eyes and touch me;
I think of you so often, believe me.

What do I do with my time?
Get active and live life;
We're so similar, we struggle with structure;
But you don't need rules when you haven't got a care;
An ideal life if there was no such thing as fear;
No labels of the 'trier', 'taker', 'leaver' or 'giver';
Everything wrong in our other life didn't manifest here;
For we are bold, invested and make our intentions clear;

Would we trust our hearts and be true believers?
Would I strengthen my mind and break stability fever?
We're intelligent and aligned, no need for a seer:
Seriously asking yourself, "Could I build my future with her?"

What happens next? Don't listen to the rumours and jeers;
Forget the rest of them, honey, and come near;
Hold me close and whisper truths in my ear;
Time won't preen us apart if we prove our lifelong career;
If we love ourselves we can love each other.

And if we were lucky enough to have that sweet love;
A compatible lifestyle, no push comes to shove;
We'd be more than a lesson; a "shake up your world";
Overcome all our lessers; two souls now whole;
And I'd rest easy at night; a bed in your eyes;
Peacefully dreamers with no more goodbyes.

I bet in the 60s we shared this past life.

The Cold Pages

It's Just A Need; It Doesn't Mean Anything

Please don't let them

Enter you.

<u>Boundaries</u>

A choice seems free,

But payment is responsibility,

And I feel guilty,

Like I'm forced to pay,

A deal I never made.

The Best Way To Get Over Someone Is To Get Under Them

Too busy not relaxing,

To hear myself saying no.

Demonised

A baby is a baby;

They can't determine safety.

Helping Hand

You blew out my flickering flame,

When you replaced it with yours;

I'm more helpless than before.

<u>Adam & Eve</u>

Just because you're my boyfriend,

Doesn't mean I am part of your body.

Scribbled Out

I couldn't hear the song;

Too painful;

The music was open;

Lyrics hidden;

Is that how people start writing

The meanings of you?

<u>Found</u>

I feel safe

When I'm lost.

Morning Coffee

To stop the pain;

You stop the pattern.

I can't respect the past,

If it still happens;

Developed by moments;

They're not certain;

Change your perception;

Cry;

Hate;

Realize the taste;

Move away;

Let it disassemble,

Release the weight.

Sleeping Beauty

If my eyes aren't open,
I can't give consent.

Crash Landing

Isn't it sad,

When our own arms

Won't catch us?

Penny Wise

You can evict your memories,
To clean up your life;
But if your habits don't change,
You've got a squatter inside.

Cold Hour

It's silent in my heart tonight;
The wind runs through tunnels outside,
And I fill the walls with books and TV.

I love the stillness;
Can't pretend I don't;
Have run from it before;
Believing I was a ghost;
Haunting myself;
A plague on the world;
Rushed to the city,
To become a new girl.

It was brave of me then,
To return to the stillness;
I got more than I bargained for;
Believed in witches.

It's a sad song in my heart tonight;
What I saw so clearly,
Is tiptoeing around my mind;
I'm basking in the stillness;
All my seams are seam-less;
But I'm still home inside;
It's there; not died.

What They Have to Teach Us

"Feel my heavenly caress." She said to her companion;
He faced her with strength and anticipation;
"Whatever is your desire?" He asked his mistress.

She coursed through him, and smacked him every evening;
But some days with gentler force than others;
He was a foundation, a body;
She was the nourishment; the blood making him appear sturdy;

Good were the days they were in love;
She glistened as she slid sleepily against him,
And he stood tall like a hero in a storybook;

"May you come save me, my Prince, when I have lost my foul mood."
"May you always come greet me, my love, when you travel with a heart of the
moon.
I am but Earth's child and I'll keep you safe and afloat;
And you shall grant me sensations with your voluptuous ebb and flow."

Us mere humans may dangle our feet over his arms to taste her vie;
But as we look on at their thrashing relationship, we keep at bay,
And only engage when they're at peace.

He remains when she goes away,
But she returns in patterns every day;
And no matter how it looks to us,
The manner of their relationship is brave,
For they keep on saving each other from a life that could go to waste.

With every blink of the eye, and each salt crystal that flies,
He kisses her with rough edges, allowing her someone different to stand beside;
And she keeps him out of breath all night.

If you embrace her nature she will be good to you;
If you respect his stance he will always stay true;
But if you challenge them you will surely lose,
For they don't change, so your actions must reflect on you.

Paper Aeroplane

In my youth,
I saw life as a connect the dot:
You made a move; knew what you'd get.
I didn't bare my truth,
Because if it was out,
My world might dilute,
So I encased my heart.

You were honest and clear;
With a keen eye and ear;
Shame my behaviour,
Screamed self-rejection and fear.

I didn't grasp boundaries,
Felt intruded when seen.
Swung between feeling,
Like a good or bad person;
My way of control,
Was to shut down or appease.

It may seem strange,
To pretend you're empty;
Limiting experience,
To a harmless fancy;
But I kept my thoughts in a place,
Where they'd belong to me only.

You taught me how,
To make a paper plane;
I followed the rules;
Tried to balance the weight;
But when it came time to launch,
It fell flat on its face.

Thanks for the lesson;
I'm no good with rules;
I only asked you to teach me,
So I could talk to you.

A Sample From The Sea

The amount of different sea creatures,
With ways of living and catching prey,
Shows how many perspectives and possibilities,
There are of being in one place;

The way they move, look and evolve;
The interactions, purposes and characters involved.

Are they all the same?
Excited by their exchange?
Does recognition in their meet and greet,
Remind them of their mission,
To live fully in their new state,
And shed old positions?

Thinking about the feelings, efforts and memories they make,
I believe there's a reason we're not the same;
Exploring growth in every detail and scope;
There's not just one, but infinite ways to be;

The truth can be found in a sample from the sea.

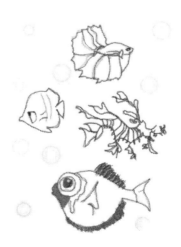

Morning Dew

If you pretend your body isn't yours,
What do you see around you?
Who is the person you wore?
What do you think they value?

If you look in the mirror,
Are you surprised?
Are you having fun moving around?
How did the former owner view their guise?
Would you change anything now?

If you look outside,
What do you see?
What clues of them are in the room?
Have you got a mission to achieve?
What of their talents impress you?

What keeps them alive?
Or did you forget?
It's easy to lose sight;
But we fell in love when we met.

Glitter

Yes, I know you;
No need to introduce yourself;
What is it you want?
We can get through this much faster.

I caught you by the eye,
And playfully rush your time;
You are declined a moment,
And get excited by your mind.

It doesn't matter, see?
Keep your steps to the beat;
We lose nothing when we falter;
Just a glimpse into an alter.

I'll leave you now,
For our exchange has spent;
Don't follow it up or hamper;
You're clinging to something else.

I've forgotten you in an hour,
But your gaze is on my back;
Strongly claiming a link,
To my blooming song tracks.

But I've left you behind;
Don't be sad;
This thing you dream will not be mine;
It isn't so bad.

Wonder what I'll do when I get home;
What stories I'll write;
Of moments like ours;
My obsession there lies.

What is it about such rhythms,
That have us rewinding?
We throw around all this glitter,
That months after we like finding.

Gem

Pink clouds and crystals;
Cloudy white, sweet smog;
Let me draw out of my heart,
All that I'd left clogged.

Your pain escaped my eyes;

I saw no life;

I saw my fear and hate;

You're a human;
You feel,
And hurt,
And stress,
Just like me;

If I'd only seen.

I'll speak to you now,
But you'll have to understand,
I'm not used to this microphone and stand.

It can only be good,
All that falls out;
Like watching sweets pour from an animal bag;
You know that's what this game is about.

I love you,
And I'm sorry.
I had no rules or words,
To place on the corners and quarries.

You held your own,
So tightly;
I was blinkered,
By inside me.

We're much the same,

Yet the value strayed;
But I'm catching up to it now,
And I'm asking it to stay.

You're a precious gem inside my chest;
Full of life before she'd revealed you;
I'd needed my sister's help,
To take those hungry breaths;

Now I see your shine like someone turned down the lights,
I'm reassured; your gift is finally in sight.

I hope I won't need to run anymore,
For you and I enrich the frame,
I'd stored away in scorn;

My young eyes couldn't understand;
They'd strained themselves bloody;
Unable to see you fully.

Just because I'd missed raw moments,
Doesn't mean our connection was stolen;
I'm beholden of the stone I kept as a child;
Now it's incandescently golden.

Kind man;
You were a kind man.
For all the faults I saw,
I forgot you were more than;

Before you were human.

When It Rains

Sometimes I can be distracted by the indoors,
And I hear it rain.

I stop what I'm doing and smile.

Outside is life;
Nature is calling.

Sometimes I'll go out and feel it on my skin;
Something inside wakes up;
Sings.

Sometimes I'll be in a bad mood,
And I'll hear it rain;

I remember what it is,
To see life outside of me;
Wonders of the world;
Joy without guarantee.

Sometimes there's thunder;
Even better.

My mood has gone and I'm happy;
Nature is my reality check;
Brings my soul to the surface;
Brings me home.

I'm thankful love in something so quiet,
Can remind me;
It doesn't matter;
I remember the blissful peace,
Of being altogether;

Sometimes I'll be wandering;
Lost or discovering,
And then it rains;
An old friend;

I'm sheltered by the water.
Something better than walking alone,
Is walking with the weather.

I won't forget my love now;
For myself or the shower;
Connecting on a deeper level with a flower.

The feeling of separation and rejection is washed away;
Instant smile on my face;
I'm full of confidence and joy,
When I'm getting soaked by the rain.

To Be Vegan

To honour your values,
Means stepping away from the world as you know it;
Everyone's home,
They know how to play it.

Relationships test me;
Never meeting those on the same path.
I build a faithful sail
On a wobbling mast.

The pain inside isn't required to love;
I've known it to be full of sacrifices,
But push comes to shove.

Thinking of others will soften the wrath;
But I want to fight for this cause with everything I have.
Confused by the feelings;
Trying to close up the distance of this universal gap.

Forgetting my needs puts me last;
Betraying my values eats at my heart.

Telling others of your most treasured truths,
To be agreed with and understood,
Then to watch them eat a cow's baby and mix a drink with a chicken's failed
motherhood.

Where's the meaning of your words gone?
Emptiness has never been a bolder person.

Alas we all know where our ease runs low;
And we can only each of us say, what we can live with at the end of the day.

Blue Organ

It hurts when a river,
Is mistaken for a lagoon;
Your excitement is insulting,
If it ignites a touch too soon;

Your sunlight was peaking;
Dancing gently on my stream;
But you weren't attentive of my nature;
Waiting until you could swim.

My appearance changes often;
I get confused by my needs;
I wish I hadn't feared pollution,
To go relying on your beams;

Now I'm feeling rippled;
Disgusted by the invasion;
I wish I hadn't tricked myself;
For now my power's fading.

I no longer want you near me;
Even if it means I'm dark and cold;
It's not worth keeping company,
If you only see them in a hole.

I hope my corruption goes;
I'm weeping wells of warning;
Support is how we stay afloat,
But check the identity you're adorning.

Safety Net

My idea of love has changed;
No more sucking in,
To each other's lives;

I am my own being,
And I only appreciate;
Valuing company.

I don't need to be obsessed over;
Loved so completely,
Possession takes over.

In fact, first sign of that,
And I'll be out the door;
I never thought that would alter;
For me, the dreamer;
Always a hand to the believers,
Because they exposed my ideas.

It's a slippery walkway,
To give emotions to someone to regulate;
It won't make you whole;
Only trigger a survival state;
Adrenaline rushing through your veins,
Because needing something,
Is great when empty balloons over-inflate.

But where's the fun in calm?
You'd give your right arm,
For them to see things your way;
But they've got their own path paved.

No explosions;
Still friction;
No waterfalls;
Just consistent.

It's not always right,
But when you present 'plights',

In your former lover's eyes,
Their love still naturally shines;

Takes me aback;
Makes me fly in new lights.

A challenging love,
Can be hot to the touch;
Feeding your thralls;
Nearly trapping your hands in the door.

But a slow building one,
Although unassuming and fallow,
Might keep you on your goals;
A heart open to faults;
A guiltless stomach full.

So perhaps the heat and the storm,
Are a baggage release;
A process so necessary,
To help your cells transform,
And rip through old beliefs.
Don't keep life entwined with death;
If a dirty window gets closed,
Open a door to enrichen your breaths.

Huh

A gulf of silence,
I dip my hand in,
Swill my fingers around,
It makes a new sound.

You're one of those;
Months can pass,
And I'll still be loosening those laces of my tight clothes.

A beat to an old rhythm,
Surfacing in present day,
A gift that keeps on giving,
Truth in vulnerability's face.

It could be another lifetime before I'd see you,
And that's what I'd need to really value,
What you gave me.

Only every now and again,
Will the light hit me.

Picket Fence

I feel like I've stepped forward,
but there's a hole in my chest,
Because my heart is in the palm of someone's hand,
A few metres back.

Build me a picket fence;
Build me;
You've made that heart dense;
I've got to clear some space;
Make it free,
For love to find me.

It's hard to let go;
Things live on much longer for me,
Even if I was the one to end them;
My heart ghosts me;
Throw it forward;
Throw my shadow into the light.

That magical point in time and space,
When dreams and reality coincide;
What's the name for that?

Our Hands Will Never Hold

"Never be apart."
But who's the conqueror today?
Trapped in a shallow pool of dismay;
Beside me you want to stand,
But you can never hold my hand.

Need a beast to hide behind,
As it eases up my mind;
I see you in a flustered rush;
Greet you in my deepest blush.

Am I afraid of my own shadow?
Round and round we go;
I once looked upon you;
Too confusing to behold.

Are you my fears?
Metaphors of my anger?
Am I capable of what you conspire?

Are you wrong?
In how many ways?
Am I a good person,
If I submit myself to shame?

The trick is to embrace you;
Give in to your persuasion;
To ignore you only strengthens,
What I spend my time escaping.

We are meant to be;
Together we make balance;
It shouldn't be taboo;
Only voicing yourself in silence.

You were exiled from my Kingdom,
When you offended all the guests;
The Queen admired your candour,
But the King found you a pest.

So I gave you less attention,
And soon you went away;
Still you show up unexpectedly,
And I cower much the same.

I look for you in suitors;
In confident female voices;
I see you in hurt children;
I'm not fooled by all pretences.

Always stay together;
Why should it be a secret?
I know I shouldn't fear you,
For I am your heart's true keeper.

That mean old shadow;
Just a scared child.
Maybe if I take you by the hand,
It'll all become worthwhile.

Hello Hope

Sometimes I doubt myself;
I'll think of consequences,
To the feelings of others,
Before I trust in what I believe;
Before I act on what I feel;
Missing information is what I heed.

Sometimes I'll wish,
For things I've missed;
I'll wonder what it means,
Or if I should pretend it means nothing;
Is that what they believe?
It's all fancy; superstition;
I'm stuck on my imagination.

But then what is that truth?
Our DNA remembers and relays sacred knowledge;
Our energies swap information;
Is a puzzle piece not a connection?

I'm still hung up on the old sequence;
Am I overlooking some substance?

What if,
It does all mean something?
What if it means something?

Hot Headed Snakes

He was steady and calm,
But lava ran through him;
Molten rock of his own making,
Outgrew him.

Took things in accordance with stability and reason;
His experiences his own,
You'd have to look closely to see them.

But what happens when he meets the girl of his equal?
In passions and depth,
Through facades versus free will.

Like two snakes circling, tail to tongue;
She believed in meaning,
He disbanded the burden.

She was raw and pure,
Radiating her feelings;
Her experiences her own but she longed for you to see them;
Vulnerable as a baby;
A Strong minded lady;
To not find her role in your life drove her crazy.

So if we put your rebelling sensibility,
And hard work, lips set,
To her magnified glances,
And free flowing, bereft,

You'll find a hard current sea,
Lifting a flippant shipwreck;

Two fire breathing dragons;

One guilty of its power,
The other with poison in its belly from the smoke down its neck.

Damming

Don't come too close;
My doors are locked;
The screen is glass,
To pretend it's not.

I won't take you literally,
So don't busy me with words;
I don't need a body,
To experience touched nerves.

I can't let you in,
Because it's in process inside;
Just how I like it;
A story to write.

Imagine you're painting,
And you're halfway along,
And someone stands watching,
Thinking you're done;

One harsh word could scar it,
And send it to bed;
It may never be attended,
If its calls can't be heard.

Yet you saw its beauty,
Alone, only you;
Until someone said different;
Which version is true?

Nothing has changed,
Except the attention it's earned;
The value of the painting,
Belongs to the first.

Should you still show it
If it won't be adored?
Is its existence reliant,
Upon receiving applause?

Or will it still live?
Humour my pen,
Because threats can't anguish,
Imaginary friends.

Am I accepted?
Maybe more than I know.
Who's building a dam?
And who's a river in flow?

It's ok to shift states;
The moon lives by phase;
You've still got the easel,
Even if it's escaping your gaze.

And those who hold space,
See more than the eye;
If you respect the exterior,
I might just let you inside.

Lighthouse Keeper

We always liked the same music,
And tv programmes;
We loved animals and dreaming;
Paint brushes in hand.

A highly wound-up piece of my heart,
That even I can't get into;
If I stroke it softly,
With no pressure,
It sometimes takes me by surprise,
When it shows me a picture.

This isn't a poem about father-daughter love,
Although it's there,
Hard to tap into,
For whatever reason.

It does not satisfy expectations,
As I didn't know what to make of you;
A wispy image shaking in the wind;
It hurts to grasp at; a straining sensation.

Blamed myself,
For my teenage fits.
We distanced,
Then you passed;
I was shards of wood and snapped sticks.

Perhaps you played an active role,
In your own way,
And I'm not seeing things clearly;
Waiting for us after school,
A close home-hub life you made;
An influence of supreme subtlety.

There was an ego hidden;
Room for misunderstandings;
You couldn't assert your feelings;
Fool's gold all abandoned.

Only mum knew your meanings;
You wouldn't answer me when I demanded them;
Was easier when we were children,
Because I didn't expect anything.

But your heart was whole;
Ready hands to hold;
Made sandwiches when I was ill;
Freedom nourished at a writer's window sill.

When it was time to integrate at school;
To fit in and change my tune;
My soul had forgotten how to sing,
And I dragged your wings down too.

You told me you'd die at 99;
It's good that now I'm teasing;
We spoke of psychics;
Bonding over spiritual healing.

Back then I couldn't make up my mind,
Of what you'd owed to me;
Not kind of my imagination,
To test and goad me.

You'd always thought I'd hit the ground with a fall,
And that's exactly what I did,
Of course;
Maybe that's why you didn't share stories;
You saw that from myself I hid;
Balancing on a punctured ball.

Either way, I still see you as a sanctuary;
The ground I tie my roots;
I still can't place our rhythm,
But I'll dance myself amused.

Family is my cherished sea;
Mum's my beaming light;
The rocks aren't what the world should be,
But you're in the lighthouse,

Watching,
Smiling with delight.

Self-Love

If a drop of rain touched you,
You'd feel it vibrate through your body;
Active and well, your spirit would soar.
Negative energy; lack of safety; drains occur;
You close up for protection,
Remaining pure.

I wouldn't have you any other way;
If you keep rebuilding yourself,
Better things will appear;
You'll attract more suitable, enhancing fixtures;
Trust your heart and release your fear.

Dream Of A Real Boy

God that fire;
The throws around my body;
My vital functions jumping;
I'm blazing,
Like I've never been alight;
Holy hell.

I wanted that core,
Of passion;

Rip me up and spit me out;
I can deal with the aftermath;
In fact I love it;
That self-growth;
You can't earn that with another,
Only myself.

I love that single life;
Not for sin,
Or virtue;
But to discover my own.

To share it is insulting,
If the stage light isn't beaming.

You were good to me;
Befriended me in my moment of need;
I had done you wrong,
But you'd carved out your spot;
Felt like you belonged.

I didn't like it;
Not one bit;

It was fantastic,
But I was erratic;
Wanted to taste life;
The fizziness and the tantric.
Then you were there,

Helping me heal but my toxicity was extracted;

Like a comfort blanket,
You were everything to me;
You opened my attic,
And what I thought of as ugly,
Was finally in flow;
I'd needed this so I could let go.

But because you waited,
I committed;
Didn't want to;
I was advised not to resist it.

If you hadn't been so familiar,
I never would have erupted;
You looked at me with care,
But inside I felt corrupted.

It wasn't made to be maintained;
There was relief when it was over.

Our friendship remained,
But I couldn't take us revolving around each other.

Stuck on you;
Trapped in a fretful zone;
My soul,
Was not at home.

I got some scissors and cut you loose;
Made a choice to get over you.
I cried every night;
It was too much, too soon.

Then you found another;
You'd met her in the summer,
But stuck with me instead;
It was only fair you bumped into her again.

It felt both wrong and right;

I was in pain but glowing;
My ambitions rose;
My talents were growing.

I needed to be an individual,
And not lean on anyone,
So I could make my own vessel,
And shoot for the sun.

All this time, I've done the same thing;
Placing poor boundaries;
Like I had to share everything.

I was wrong;
I needed the trials,
The banging of drums,
To honour my planet,
And hear my own heart thump.

The Lonely Flower

Daydreaming about lying on the grass,
And sharing secrets with a friend;
Lots of memories swarming my head,
Of friendships abandoned at the stems.

I can't wait to regather myself;
Put down the thorns and fly sprays;
I want to spend a night with old lovers,
And chat honestly with acquaintances.

My garden was filled with all colours and shapes;
When I'm a single flower,
I appreciate sharing the space.

I know I can put my hand in yours;
There's a gate always open;
When the wind changes course,
I'll walk without hesitation.

Charity Shop

I thought of you all that time;
From winter to summer;
Wanting that closure I was denied.
I bit the bullet and text you;
Heart fluttering with panic;
I feared hell,
But you welcomed me past it.

There we were again,
As if no fire had scorched us;
I walked with you across the shore;
Talking as though we'd resurfaced.

You spoke as if you knew me well;
So innocent;
But something was lurking;
A creature in a closed shell, returning.

I felt unsafe before long;
You said your actions had good intentions,
But I struggled to belong,
Because I didn't.

A disagreement soon came,
After we tried to recapture chess games;
I had a lighter aim;
No more mental peacocking to win your acclaim.

I attacked your character because of your behaviour;
It defeated the point of your considerate words;
I'd failed to speak my nerves;
And all illusions emerged.

You didn't like it,
When I expressed upset;
You blamed me but I ignored you;
Tired of pushing the concept.

A few days later, I caved and tried to explain;

But you were gone; a flippant ghost like me before you;
Recycled rain.

I bought a book to explain you to me;
It did a great deal and gave me relief.
Like a drug, you left me with an open vent;
I had to go back so I could get a neat end.

After two weeks, I begged for an explanation;
That closure I deserved;
You had just wanted to leave it,
But thought better of the caused hurt.

I don't remember now what was said,
But I know that I was never quite heard,
Over the noise of your coping mechanisms,
And depleting reserves.

The best thing that happened was me losing patience;
Because in order to risk my fear,
Of becoming a bad person,
I had to stop putting up with that nonsense.

I gave up the guilt to take action;
I gained insight into the feeling of being a well-rounded person.

The next free opportunity,
I took the gifts you gave,
And the Queen chess piece I'd saved,
To a charity shop, away.

The cashier picked up my items like they were theatrical props,
Expecting me to laugh and clap;
I didn't find it funny,
How my moment was stopped.

I didn't ask you to stay;
I allowed myself to hate;
To ventilate;
I discovered more puzzle pieces,
for the full picture of my face.

But I'll still wish you well,
From our separate bean stalks;
To honour myself,
I'll sharpen my forte.

Hoarding Diamonds

The people I encounter,
Know how to let things go;
My fear and pain linger;
It's almost out of my control;

I get the impression this isn't normal,
But that doesn't stop it being;
Maybe it's my source of magic,
To master my art of storytelling.

Thank you for reading.

Letter to the reader

If this book can show you anything, it's that we aren't always going to feel sure of ourselves; like we fit in; like we know what's right or wrong, or at home in our own bodies. Feelings can be hard to handle but regret, fear and shame are an absence of self-love.

I want you to know that you are deeply loved, down to the very core of your soul. It's ok to make mistakes and it's unavoidable. They make your life interesting, wise, funny, and inspiring. You've got a lot to show for yourself and fuel behind you to do it.

It's ok if you feel incapable or fragile and don't want to step outside today; you've got to do what best serves you.

It's ok if you're angry, sad, annoyed, disgusted, or scared. You have every right to be. I want you to know that you deserve to be here and it's understandable to feel how you feel. Own your space and recognise you're important.

We don't always know what's to come in our lives and this can knock us off balance. If we don't feel put together or prepared, our worries can rage out of control. But you're strong and capable of exploring the unknown. Think about how the unknown will be after you come its way.

You never have to do anything you don't want to do so don't be afraid of your own power. If people mind your protests, then they don't have your best interests at heart. Love is setting boundaries so you can honour yourself. Always be honest with yourself about how you feel.

I want you to know that you will always be forgiven because we do the best we know how to, and we will always have a place to belong. You deserve to be respected and treated with care. May you always find the courage to carve your own path and have faith that you are thought of.

It's inspiring to see people shine doing what they love. You have brought something unique into this world and I'm excited to learn your spirit. May you always feel free to express it and bring your light into our lives.

With my highest and purest love,
Grace.

Printed in Great Britain
by Amazon

60658940R00045